success

These quotations were gathered lovingly but unscientifically over several years and/or contributed by many friends or acquaintances. Some arrived, and survived in our files, on scraps of paper and may therefore be imperfectly worded or attributed. To the authors, contributors and original sources, our thanks, and where appropriate, our apologies.—The editors

CREDITS

Compiled by Kobi Yamada
Designed by Steve Potter

ISBN: 1-888387-69-6

Printed in China

If you know you want it, have it.

GITA BELLIN

Believe it!
High
expectations
are the
key to
everything.

SAM WALTON

Some succeed because they are destined to; most succeed because they are determined to.

ANATOLE FRANCE

I think I can break the odds.

JOSE FERNANDEZ

WE KNOW WHAT WE ARE,
BUT KNOW NOT WHAT WE MAY BE.

WILLIAM SHAKESPEARE

FROM SMALL

BEGINNINGS

COME GREAT

THINGS.

PROVERB

THE
BEGINNING
IS ALWAYS
TODAY.

MARY WOLLSTONECRAFT

Go and wake up your luck.

PERSIAN PROVERB

I've found that
luck is quite predictable.
If you want more luck,
take more chances.
Be more active.
Show up more often.

BRIAN TRACY

The one who takes a chance, who walks the line between the known and the un-known, who won't accept failure, will succeed.

SUSAN FIELDER

Decide that
you want it
more than you
are afraid of it.

BILL COSBY

THE FIRST STEP
TOWARDS
GETTING SOMEWHERE
IS TO DECIDE THAT
YOU ARE NOT
GOING
TO STAY
WHERE YOU ARE.

J . PIERPONT MORGAN

HAVE A GO.
ANYBODY CAN DO IT.

ALAN PARKER

If you're looking
for a big
opportunity,
seek out
a big problem.

SIMON BLEY

Until you try,

you don't know

what you can do.

HENRY JAMES

GOING FROM—TOWARD;
   IT IS THE HISTORY OF EVERY ONE OF US.

H E N R Y   D A V I D   T H O R E A U

Inspiration follows aspiration.

RABINDRANATH TAGORE

YOU MISS
100 PERCENT
OF THE
SHOTS YOU
NEVER TAKE.

WAYNE GRETZKY

He who would learn to fly one day must first learn to stand and walk and run and climb and dance; one cannot fly into flying.

FRIEDRICH NIETZSCHE

WHEN I MAKE UP MY MIND

TO DO SOMETHING, I MAKE

SURE IT HAPPENS. YOU CAN'T

WAIT FOR THE PHONE TO RING.

YOU HAVE TO RING THEM.

WILSON SMITH

Three essentials:
Know what
you're doing.
Love what
you're doing.
Believe in what
you're doing.

STEVE MUSSEAU

NO BIRD SOARS TOO HIGH IF HE
SOARS WITH HIS OWN WINGS.

WILLIAM BLAKE

The difference between the impossible and the possible lies in a person's determination.

TOMMY LASORDA

Tomorrow belongs to the people who prepare for it today.

MALCOLM X

You must be ready

not only to take

opportunities,

but to make them.

ROD MOORE

Nothing can add more power to your life than concentrating all your energies on a limited set of targets.

NIDO QUBEIN

WE AIM ABOVE THE MARK
TO HIT THE MARK.

RALPH WALDO EMERSON

In great
attempts it
is glorious
even to fail.

CASSIU LONGINUS

We are all failures,
at least all the best of us are.

JAMES M. BARRIE

It's supposed to be hard; if it wasn't hard, everyone would do it. The hard is what makes it great.

TOM HANKS

GUTS GET YOU THERE.

B.C.   FORBES

Being in the right place
at the right time
won't make you
a success—unless
you're ready.
The important
question is:
"Are you ready?"

JOHNNY CARSON

Why let others define success for you?

Here are two insights that

can allow you to live successfully

in your own way every day:

1) Compete only with your own best self.

2) Steadily move toward your

own worthwhile goals.

MARTHA REID

Though the road you're walking may be well-traveled, that does not necessarily mean it is leading to your destination.

UNKNOWN

Hold yourself to a higher standard than anybody else expects of you.

HENRY WARD BEECHER

When we
strive to become
better than
we are,
everything around
us becomes
better, too.

KOBI YAMADA

I will study and get ready and

someday my chance will come.

ABRAHAM LINCOLN

The secret of success
is constancy of purpose.

BENJAMIN DISRAELI

When you are inspired by some great purpose, some extra-ordinary project, all your thoughts break their bonds, your mind transcends limitations, your consciousness expands in every direction, and you find yourself in a new, great and wonderful world. Dormant forces, faculties and talents come alive, and you find yourself to be a greater person by far than you ever dreamed yourself to be.

PATANJALI

If error is corrected whenever

it is recognized as such, the

path of error is the path of truth.

HANS REICHENBACK

BETWEEN
THE FAILURE AND THE
MASTERPIECE,
THE DISTANCE IS ONE
MILLIMETER.

PAUL GAUGIN

It's the constant and determined effort that breaks down all resistance and sweeps away all obstacles.

CLAUDE M BRISTOL

When nothing seems to help

I go and look at the stonecutter

hammering away at his rock

perhaps a hundred times without

so much as a crack showing in it.

Yet at the hundred and first blow

it will split in two, and I know it

was not that blow that did it—

but all that had gone before.

MILO SCHULTZ

History has demonstrated that the most notable winners usually encountered heart breaking obstacles before they triumphed. They won because they refused to become discouraged by their defeats.

BERTIE C. FORBES

CLEAR YOUR MIND OF CAN'T.

SAMUEL JOHNSON

PUT YOUR HEART, MIND, INTELLECT AND SOUL TO EVEN YOUR SMALLEST ACTS. THIS IS THE SECRET TO SUCCESS.

SCOTT LIPKE

Working together, ordinary people

can perform extraordinary feats.

They can push things that come

into their hands a little higher

up, a little farther on towards

the heights of excellence.

B. J. MARSHALL

You cannot stay on the summit forever; you have to come down again...so why bother in the first place? Just this: what is above knows what is below, but what is below does not know what is above.

RENE DAUMAL

There are no limits but the sky. Believe.

HARRIET MITCHELL

THIS ONE STEP,
CHOOSING A GOAL AND STICKING TO IT,
CHANGES EVERYTHING.

S C O T T   R E E D

From a certain point onward there is no longer any turning back. That is the point that much be reached.

FRANK KAFKA

The real moment
of success
is not the moment
apparent
to the crowd.

GEORGE BERNARD SHAW

Every vital organization owes its birth and life to an exciting and daring idea.

JAMES B. CONANT

Innovate or evaporate.

JIM HIGGINS

Dreams are necessary to life.

ANAIS NIN

Every moment is a

sacred moment,

and every action,

when imbued with

dedication and commitment

to benefit all beings,

is a sacred act.

DHYANI YWAHOO

the good life™

Celebrating the joy of living fully.

Also available from Compendium Publishing are these spirited companion books in The Good Life series of great quotations:

yes!
refresh
moxie
hero
friend
heart
spirit
joy
thanks

These books may be ordered directly
from the publisher (800) 914-3327.
But please try your local bookstore first!

www.compendiuminc.com

The secret of achievement is not to let what you're doing get to you before you get to it.

KOBI YAMADA